BOOKS BY
Jean-Claude van Itallie

THE SERPENT   1969

AMERICA HURRAH   1968

The Serpent

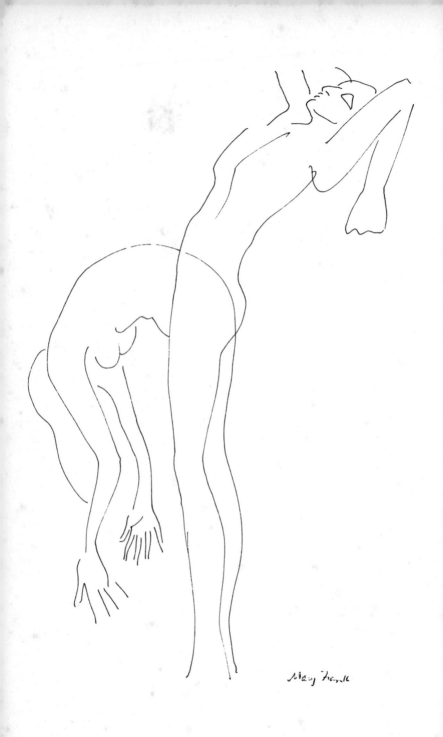

The Serpent

A CEREMONY WRITTEN BY

Jean-Claude van Itallie

IN COLLABORATION WITH

The Open Theater

UNDER THE DIRECTION OF

Joseph Chaikin

ATHENEUM   NEW YORK   1969

To the memory of Roger H. Klein

THE SERPENT, *a ceremony created by the Open Theater under the direction of* JOSEPH CHAIKIN, *assisted by* ROBERTA SKLAR, *words and structure* by JEAN-CLAUDE VAN ITALLIE, *opened in Rome at the Teatro del Arte on May 2, 1968.*

The Open Theater company of actors:

JOYCE AARON	JAYNE HAYNES
JAMES BARBOSA	RALPH LEE
RAYMOND BARRY	DOROTHY LYMAN
JENN BEN-YAKOV	PETER MALONEY
SHAMI CHAIKIN	ELLEN SCHINDLER
BRENDA DIXON	TINA SHEPARD
RON FABER	BARBARA VANN
CYNTHIA HARRIS	LEE WORLEY
PHILIP HARRIS	PAUL ZIMET

The arrangers of sounds: STANLEY WALDEN *and* RICHARD PEASLEE

Associate: PATRICIA COOPER

The stage manager: KEN GLICKFELD

The administrative director: RICHARD SNYDER

Costumes by: GWEN FABRICANT

From the Playwright

Theater is not electronic. Unlike movies and unlike television, it does require the live presence of both audience and actors in a single space. This is the theater's uniquely important advantage and function, its original religious function of bringing people together in a community ceremony where the actors are in some sense priests or celebrants, and the audience is drawn to participate with the actors in a kind of eucharist.

Where this is the admitted function of theater the playwright's work is not so much to "write a play" as to "construct a ceremony" which can be used by the actors to come together with their audience. Words are a part of this ceremony, but not necessarily the dominant part, as they are not the dominant part either in a formal religious ceremony. The important thing is what is happening between the audience and the action. At each point in constructing the ceremony the playwright must say to himself: "What is the audience experiencing now? At what point are they on their journey and where are they to be brought to next?" The "trip" for the audience must be as carefully structured as any ancient mystery or initiation. But the form must reflect contemporary thought processes. And we don't think much in a linear fashion. Ideas overlap, themes recur, archetypal figures and events transform from shape to shape as they dominate our minds.

The creation of this piece was an exploration of certain ideas and images that seem to dominate our minds and lives. The only criterion, finally, of whether or not to follow an impulse in the piece was: Did it work for us or not, in our lives, in our thoughts, and in the playing on the stage.

A large part in the creation of the ceremony was "letting go." For my part, I let go a great many words, characters and scenes. And most painfully I let go certain rigid structural concepts I had invented to replace the linear ones of a conventional play. But whatever was good of these—a funeral, a Catholic mass, an LSD trip, an inquisition, a modern mystery play—remains within the structure of the present ceremony. And so too, lengthy discussions, improvisations, and even unstated common feelings within the company remain somewhere within the final piece—in fact more, probably, than even we can remember.

When other acting groups want to perform *The Serpent* I hope that they will use the words and movements only as a skeleton on which they will put their own flesh. Because *The Serpent* is a ceremony reflecting the minds and lives of the people performing it. What I would like to think is that we have gone deep enough into ourselves to find and express some notions, some images, some feelings which will bring the actors together with the audience, and that these images, these ideas, these feelings, will be found to be held in common.

Jean-Claude van Itallie

From the Director

All entertainment is instructive. It instructs the sensibility. It needn't give information in order to instruct. In fact, information can more easily be rejected than the ambiance of the entertainment.

Within the theater it is often believed that except for the concerns of the particular character he is playing, the less an actor knows about the implications of a work, the better. In a work like *The Serpent* the actor must understand as much as can be understood. Here the ideas in the piece are as important to the actor's understanding as are his individual character motivations. Since the strength of the production rests on the power of the ensemble of actors, the ensemble must address itself to the questions and images which make up *The Serpent*. The most hazardous and rewarding problem in a group effort such as this one is to find communal points of reference.

*　　*　　*

Because the main part of the piece is taken from a narrative, the story of Genesis in the Bible, it is important that the group of actors first look for images which come close to their own early pictures of these stories. The more faithful their images are to their own garden-in-the-mind, to Adam and Eve, etc., the more Jean-Claude van Itallie's text will emerge. *The text follows the narrative of Genesis, and is at the same time a repudiation of its assumptions, thus forming a dialectic.* What is deeply engaging in the biblical mythology is the discovery that its assumptions are even now the hidden bases of a lot of our making of choices.

The text gives a structure for the playing out of the story, and includes places for the company to improvise. Performing an improvisation is seldom successful without a framework to contain the kinetic happening—that which is going on in the room in a non-verbal, non-literal way. The springboard of the improvisation is within the narrative, such as in the ecstasy of Adam and Eve after the apple has been bitten. But once the actors are in the house playing out the exploration of the ecstasy, there is the other reality of people-players and audience—and here is where the delicate and mysterious encounter takes

place. That encounter is not "made," but "permit-
ted." It is not performed at that moment, but let be.
It is caused neither by the actor nor by the audience,
but by the silence between them.

The actors consciously confront the full bewilderment of people together in a room. Some of the
audience are pleased at the shift of focus from the
stage to the whole room as a larger stage. Some of
the audience have been disgusted with the whole
proceedings from the start, and here may express it.
And others in the audience are also aware of their
own bewilderment. Within the narrative are guide-
posts which are springboards for the actors to give
form to this otherwise formless encounter. The aim
in the improvised parts is not simply to assess the
players' or the audience's attitudes. The confrontation is with that delicate but powerful pulse of people assembled in the same room. For this reason it
is the rhythm and dynamic responses, rather than
the confrontation of attitudes between the actor and
the audience, which are important. This special task
is possible in the particular context of the *anony-
mous intimacy* between players and audience, and
through it the main theme which is the confrontation of our mortality.

* * *

The role of the four women who make up the chorus is multiple. They are, to the audience, hostesses. They are narrator and chorus. They are contemporary widows mourning "the good life." They introduce ideas which are thematic perspectives. They bring everything into question by juxtaposing the worldly with the otherworldly. They "de-mystify" by making common, and yet untenable, statements. They answer questions implied in the rest of the text by further questions, continually intruding on answers to bring into focus the unanswerable.

It would be difficult to overstress the importance of the group effort. In usual theater situations the text is there, and the director follows out his own plan. But in *The Serpent* the text invites all those working on it to create what will happen on stage. The director is the agent through whom the work finds its final plan, but he does not fix anything in his mind before the work begins. The actors collaborate fully, introducing images and possibilities, some of which they will themselves eventually embody on the stage. The collaboration requires that each person address to himself the major questions posited in the material: what are my own early pictures of Adam and Eve and the serpent, of the Garden of Eden, of Cain and Abel? These questions deal with a personal remembered "first time." They are the questions we stopped asking after childhood. We stopped asking them because they were unanswerable (even though we gave or guessed at answers), and later we substituted "adult" answerable questions for them. The group must also go into these deeply dramatic questions of the "first man," "first woman," "first discovery of sex," and also into the character of God in the Old Testament. I would state that the premise of the piece is that Man made God in his own image, and held up this God to determine his own, Man's, limits.

When these questions are alive to the company of actors, there is in any of them a dangerous point when discussion must stop and the questions must be brought to the stage in terms of improvisatory actions. There are two main values in working on a piece in this way, collaboratively. One is the affirming discovery of finding deep common references. It takes time to reach these; the cliché references all need to come out first. And the second value is the astonishing power there is in the performance of an actor who is actually playing out an image which he himself introduced.

*　*　*

The first steps of collaborative work, then, are to open up and develop a vocabulary of image and action. Later the director becomes more important. He must find ways to select the most cogent from among possible images; he must enlarge any particular image through more specific demands of voice and movement; he must redefine the actors' intentions when they become lost; and he must discover ways to sustain the freshness of successive performances. That part of the work which is a combination of both fixed and improvised-for-the-night must be set up with a carefully thought-out balance, so as to make possible its existence anew each time in the particular room in which it is played. Also, the single action which has been finally chosen for each part of each scene must be a formal articulation of the one choice selected from among many, the one phrase-of-action which represents the essential impulse of the scene.

Why is *The Serpent* a ceremony? What kind of ceremony is it? It is one in which the actors and audience confront the question: where are we at in relation to where we've been? The four women of the chorus go back again and again to references about "the beginning" and "the middle." Anything may have been possible in the beginning, but now we've made the choice, and that choice excludes other possibilities. It makes those choices which are still possible fewer. The ceremony celebrates this point in time: now. We can't remake the past. *The Serpent* insists on our responsibility of acknowledging that we have already gone in a particular direction. It says: where are we at? What are the boundaries we adhere to, and how have they become fixed?

In *The Serpent* the point of crossing a boundary, such as when Eve eats the apple, is a point of transformation, and the whole company crosses a boundary. Because when even one person crosses a forbidden line, nothing is the same for anyone after that.

Joseph Chaikin

Illustrations

.

Drawing facing title page by Mary Frank

1 Photographs by Peter Bergh and Freddy Tornberg.
From left to right: Phil Harris, Jenn Ben-Yakov
(*partly hidden*), Ron Faber, Barbara Vann, Lee
Worley (*in background*), Joyce Aaron (*in background*). page 11

2 Photograph by Peter Bergh and Freddy Tornberg.
From left to right: Jayne Haynes, Tina Shepard, Phil
Harris, Brenda Dixon, Dorothy Lyman. *page* 19

3 Photograph by Peter Bergh and Freddy Tornberg.
From left to right: Tina Shepard, Paul Zimet (*partly
obscured*), Phil Harris (*on floor*), James Barbosa,
Ron Faber, Peter Maloney, Raymond Barry, Ralph
Lee. *page* 25

4 Photograph by Peter Bergh and Freddy Tornberg.
From left to right: Shami Chaikin (*seated in background*), Tina Shepard, James Barbosa, Ron Faber
(*partly obscured*), Ralph Lee, Peter Maloney.

page 33

5 Photograph by Peter Bergh and Freddy Tornberg.
From left to right: Ellen Schindler, Dorothy Lyman,
Ralph Lee. *page* 45

The Serpent

Warm-up and Procession

In all parts of the theater, including the aisle, the stage and the balcony, the actors warm up. Each does what physical exercises best prepare him for playing. The lights dim slowly and not completely. Each actor wears a costume that seems natural on him particularly, of colorful and easily falling materials that flatter the movement of his body. The total effect, when the company moves together, is kaleidoscopic. The actress who will play Eve wears a simply cut short white dress, and Adam old khaki pants and a shirt with no collar. None of the others is costumed for a particular role. As no one wears any shoes but tights or ballet slippers, a dropcloth for the stage is desirable.

After a few minutes the actors begin to move around the theater in a procession led by an actor who taps out a simple marching rhythm on a bongo drum. The players don't use their voices, but they explore every other sound that can be made by the human body—slapping oneself, pounding one's chest, etc. The actors also use simple and primitive musical instruments during the procession. During some later scenes an actor may accompany the stage action with the repeated sound of a single note on one of these instruments. The procession appears to be one of medieval mummers, and sounds like skeletons on the move. All at once all stop in a freeze. This happens three times during the procession. During a freeze each actor portrays one of various possible motifs from the play such as: the sheep, the serpent, the president's wife's reaching gesture, Adam's movement, Cain's waiting movement, Eve's movement, the heron, and the old people. In countries outside the United States where it is thought that not everyone will immediately recognize all events in the piece, at these motif moments actors shout out the names King and Kennedy.

Transitions from a scene to the next will be done rythmically, in the character of one scene or of the following, as a slow transformation or "dissolve," or completely out of character with the audience merely watching the actor go to his next place. Each transition is slightly different, but pre-determined.

The Doctor

When the procession is nearly over, the doctor detaches himself from it. A victim, a woman, from among the actors is carried over by two actors and placed on a table formed by three other actors. The doctor stands behind the table. He speaks in a kind of chant. His movements are slow and ritualistic. The rest of the actors, watching, will provide stylized sounds for the operation. A gunshot will be heard once in a while. We will already have heard the gunshot a couple of times during the end of the procession.

DOCTOR

Autopsy:
With a single stroke of the cleaver
The corpse is split open.

Actors make cutting sound from the backs of their throats

The fatty tissues
Fall away
In two yellow folds.

DOCTOR

In a corpse
The blood is black
And does not flow.
In a living person
The blood is black
And flows
From the liver
To the spine, and from
There to the heart
And the brain.
To penetrate the skull
We shave the head,
And cut out a disk of flesh
The shape of a half moon.

Actors make the sound of the saw

We inject the exposed bone
With a steel needle

And push air into the skull
To look into the brain.
Then with a diamond drill
We enter the bone.

Actors make the sound of teeth nibbling

And nibble at the opening
With a hammer, chisel and knife.
The brain is cream-colored.
It is a balance of chemicals.
Thought is effected
By traveling electrons.

Gunshot

During a brain operation
Pressing at this point
With a knife
Causes live patients
To exclaim at sudden memories.
If we press here
We get fear.

Gunshot

The patient, who so far has been lying fairly still,
climbs off the table and comes slowly toward the
audience in a state of extreme bodily tension, making a soundless appeal.

7

The Doctor

In gunshot wounds
Infection ensues
Unless an operation
Is undertaken immediately.
We excise the wound,
And suck out bits of bone
And diffluent brain matter.
If the patient survives
He may live for weeks
Or months
Or years.

The four women of the chorus make the same small
long scream at the backs of their throats that they
will make when we later see Abel's ghost.

He functions barely.
He is unconscious.
Or semi-conscious.
We don't know.
We clean him,
And feed him.
But there is no measure
To what degree
The mind imagines, receives, or dreams.

8

Kennedy-King Assassination

A cheering crowd forms in a semi-circle at the back of the stage. Using four chairs, or sitting on the floor if the stage is raked enough, four actors, two men and two women, sit in the car as the central characters in the assassination of President John F. Kennedy. The governor and his wife are in front. The President and his wife are in the back seat exactly as in all the newspaper pictures. They are waving. The crowd, moving from one side of the stage to the other behind them, gives the same impression of movement as in a film when the scenery is moved behind what is supposed to be a "moving" car. When the crowd moves the first time, one figure is left to the side: the assassin. Another figure stands behind the crowd, and does not move with it. Again, everyone but the people in the car is facing the audience. The people in the car look at the audience, smile at them as if they were the crowd. The events which are the actual assassination are broken down into a count of twelve, as if seen on a slowed-down silent film. Within this count all the things which we are told factually happened, happen:

1: All four wave.
2: President is shot in the neck.
3: Governor is shot in the shoulder.
4: President is shot in the head. Governor's wife pulls her husband down and covers him with her body.
5: President falls against his wife.
6: President's wife begins to register something is wrong. She looks at her husband.
7: She puts her hands on his head.
8: She lifts her knee to put his head on it.
9: She looks into the front seat.
10: She begins to realize horror.
11: She starts to get up.
12: She begins to crawl out the back of the open car, and to reach out her hand.

Immediately after that, the numbers are started again. The numbers have been actually shouted aloud by guards who come down toward the front of the stage and kneel, their backs to the audience. Then the count is made a third time, backward this time. The crowd reactions are also backward, as if a

film of these events were being run backward. Then the guards call out numbers from one to twelve at random, and the people in the crowd, as well as the characters in the car, assume the positions they had at the time of the particular number being called. The blank-faced assassin has simply mimed shooting a rifle at the count of two. He faces the audience, too. The action in the car continues, as if the count from one to twelve were going on perpetually, but we no longer hear the guards shouting. The crowd, aside from the assassin, forms a tight group at the rear of the right side of the stage. They face the audience. The four women of the chorus are in the front. The crowd shouts and marches very slowly toward the front.

At first, however, we have not understood what they are shouting. The shout is broken down into first vowels, second vowels, center consonants and end consonants. Each of four sections of the crowd has been assigned one part. The shout is repeated four times, each time through adding one of the four parts.

CROWD SHOUT

I was not involved.
I am a small person.

I hold no opinion.
I stay alive.

Then everyone on stage freezes, and the figure at the back quietly speaks words like the actual ones of Dr. Martin Luther King:

KING

Though we stand in life at midnight,
I have a dream.
He's allowed me
To go to the mountaintop,
And I've looked over.
I've seen the promised land.
I have a dream
That we are, as always,
On the threshold of a new dawn,
And that we shall all see it together.

The crowd continues its shout, building up the other stanzas as it did the previous one, but the words are still not completely clear. The characters in the car continue their slow-motion actions.

CROWD SHOUT

I mind my own affairs.
I am a little man.

13

I lead a private life.
I stay alive.

I'm no assassin.
I'm no president.
I don't know who did the killing.
I stay alive.

I keep out of big affairs.
I am not a violent man.
I am very sorry, still
I stay alive.

At times we have been able to make out the words of the President's wife which she has been speaking on count twelve as she reaches out.

PRESIDENT'S WIFE
I've got his brains in my—

The last time through the whole shout, we hear each section of the crowd emphasizing its own part, while the assassin, who has been standing on one side, facing the audience and going through, silently, the agonies of having been himself shot, speaks the words with the others, clearly.

14

CROWD AND ASSASSIN

I was not involved.
I am a small person.
I hold no opinions.
I stay alive.

I mind my own affairs.
I am a little man.
I lead a private life.
I stay alive.

I'm no assassin.
I'm no president.
I don't know who did the killing.
I stay alive.

I keep out of big affairs.
I am not a violent man.
I am very sorry, still
I stay alive.

The Garden

Everyone's breath comes short and heavy and rhythmically, as if in surprise. The four chorus women dressed in black detach themselves from the rest of the group and in short spurts of movement and speech go to the downstage right area, facing the audience.

FIRST WOMAN OF THE CHORUS
I no longer live in the beginning.

SECOND WOMAN OF THE CHORUS
I've lost the beginning.

THIRD WOMAN OF THE CHORUS
I'm in the middle,
Knowing.

THIRD AND FOURTH WOMEN OF THE CHORUS
Neither the end
Nor the beginning.

16

FIRST WOMAN

I'm in the middle.

SECOND WOMAN

Coming from the beginning.

THIRD AND FOURTH WOMEN

And going toward the end.

In the meantime, others are forming the creatures in the garden of Eden. They, too, emanate from the same communal "first breath." Many of the creatures are personal, previously selected by each actor as expressing an otherwise inexpressible part of himself. For the audience, perhaps the heron has the most identifiable reality. He moves about gently, tall, proud, in slow spurts; he stands on one foot, moves his wings slightly, occasionally, and makes a soft "brrring" noise. Other creatures become distinguishable. The serpent is formed by five (male) actors all writhing together in a group, their arms, legs, hands, tongues, all moving.

The chorus women have repeated their "in the beginning" lines from above. They speak these lines as a secret to the audience.

*   *   *

There is a sense of awe about the whole creation of the garden. The two human creatures also become discernible. As Eve sits up and sees the world, she screams in amazement. The sound of her scream is actually made by one of the four chorus women. They are also Eve. They think of themselves as one person, and any one of them at this moment might reflect Eve.

Adam falls asleep. The heron and the serpent are now more clearly discernible from the other creatures. The creatures play with themselves and each other quietly, in awe. The serpent is feeling out the environment with hands and mouths and fingers. There is nothing orgiastic about the garden—on the contrary, there is the restraint of curious animals in a strange environment.

Eve and the Serpent

SERPENT 1: Is it true?

SERPENT 2: Is it true

SERPENT 3: That you and he,

SERPENT 4: You and he

SERPENT 4 AND 5: May do anything?

SERPENT 2: Anything in the garden you want to do?

SERPENT 1: Is that true?

EVE: We may do anything
Except one thing.

FIRST WOMAN OF THE CHORUS:
We may do anything
Except one thing.

In the dialogue between Eve and the serpent the first of the chorus women echoes Eve's lines, but with the emphasis placed on different words. The four

20

chorus women look at the audience as if it were the serpent in front of them. The serpent speaks and hisses to Eve with all his five mouths. Care must be taken by the actors playing the serpent that all the words are heard distinctly, despite overlap in speaking. Eve is almost in a state of tremor at being alive. The serpent is seducing her with his even greater aliveness, as well as with the intellectual argument. As Eve comes closer to being in the state the serpent is in, her movements begin to imitate the serpent's, and she, finally, is seducing him, too. Some of the other actors are now seated on a bench facing the audience, at the back of the stage where they sit, and rest, and pay attention to the action. This is where those who are not playing a particular scene will always go—none of the actors will ever actually leave the stage. During Eve's dialogue with the serpent, only the heron and one or two other animals in the garden are upright, but they do not distract our attention. The serpent is not only the serpent, he is also the tree, and he holds apples.

SERPENT 2: What one thing?
EVE: We are not allowed to eat from the tree.
FIRST WOMAN: We are not allowed
To eat from the tree.

SERPENT 3: Not allowed to eat?

EVE: We may not even touch it.
WOMAN: We may not even touch it.

SERPENT 1: Not even touch?
SERPENT 4 AND 5: Not touch?
SERPENT 5: Why not even touch?

EVE: Adam said I would die.
WOMAN: Adam said I would die.

The serpent is gently surrounding her until she has touched him without her realizing it.

SERPENT 3: If you—
SERPENT 4: If you touch—
SERPENT 4 AND 5: If you touch the tree—
SERPENT 1: Adam said
SERPENT 2: If you touch the tree
SERPENT 4 AND 5: If you even touch the tree
You will die—
SERPENT 1: But—
SERPENT 2: But—
SERPENT 3: But—

Eve realizes her back is against the tree.

SERPENT 5: Have you died?
SERPENT 4 (*whispering*): Have you died?

EVE: I don't know.
WOMAN: I don't know.

SERPENT 2: You touched the tree.
SERPENT 2 AND 3: And you haven't died.
SERPENT 4: You haven't died.

EVE: But Adam said—
WOMAN: But Adam said—

SERPENT 1: Oh, Adam said
SERPENT 2: Adam said, Adam said . . .

SERPENT 1 AND 2: Listen.
SERPENT 2 AND 3: Answer me this.
SERPENT 5 (*overlapping the others*): This.
SERPENT 4: Could it?
SERPENT 3: Could it hurt more
To eat than to touch?
SERPENT 5: To eat than to touch?
SERPENT 1: Could it?

23

EVE: It is forbidden.

WOMAN: It is forbidden.

SERPENT 2: Who has forbidden it?

SERPENT 1: Who?

EVE: God.

WOMAN: God.

SERPENT 4: And why?

SERPENT 5: Why has he forbidden it?

SERPENT 4: Why?

SERPENT 3: Why does he set limits

SERPENT 2 AND 3: Against you and Adam?

SERPENT 1: Think.

SERPENT 2: Is the fruit God's property?

SERPENT 3: Is it?

SERPENT 1: He says Adam and Eve may not eat.
But are Adam and Eve
Guests in this garden?

SERPENT 2: Are they guests?

SERPENT 1: Don't they live here?

SERPENT 3: May they not eat where they want?

EVE (*turning away*): I don't know.

WOMAN: I don't know.

SERPENT 5: Also, also haven't you

SERPENT 4 AND 5: Haven't you noticed

SERPENT 4: That the younger always have rule
Over the elder creation?

SERPENT 2: Haven't you noticed,
and aren't you afraid?

SERPENT 1: Aren't you afraid
And hadn't you better hurry

SERPENT 1 AND 2: And eat the fruit now
Before the next comes to rule
Over you?

EVE: I'm not afraid.

WOMAN: I'm not afraid.

SERPENT (*to itselves*) 1: She's not afraid.

SERPENT 2: Why should she be?

SERPENT 3: How could she be?

SERPENT 4: How?

SERPENT 5: She couldn't be,
She doesn't know.

SERPENT 4: Doesn't know what?

SERPENT 3: Doesn't know she exists.

SERPENT 4: Why doesn't she know it?

SERPENT 3: Because she hasn't eaten.

SERPENT 2: If she'd eaten, she'd know.

SERPENT 1: Know what?

SERPENT 4: What worlds she would know
If she ate.

SERPENT 5: What worlds?

SERPENT 1: If she ate she would know

SERPENT 1 AND 2: And if she knew

SERPENT 1 AND 2 AND 3: She could—

EVE: What?

WOMAN: What?

SERPENT 4: You don't know

SERPENT 5: Because you haven't eaten.

EVE: Do you know?

WOMAN: Do you know?

SERPENT 2: I don't know.

SERPENT 1: I don't.

SERPENT 3: But I can imagine.

SERPENT 4: Imagine.

SERPENT 5: Imagine.

EVE: But, is what you can imagine
What will be?

WOMAN: But, is what you can imagine
What will be?

SERPENT 1 AND 2: How can you know
Until you eat?
SERPENT 5: How can I know?
SERPENT 4: How can I know until you eat?
SERPENT 1: This garden
SERPENT 2: All these animals and these plants
SERPENT 2 AND 3: Were once only imagined.

EVE: Shall I risk losing all these?
WOMAN: Shall I risk losing all these?

SERPENT 1: It may be.
SERPENT 2: It may be that no garden
SERPENT 4: Is better than this one.
SERPENT 5: This garden.
SERPENT 4: It may be.
SERPENT 2: But you won't know,
SERPENT 1: You can't know
Until you eat.
SERPENT 2: How could you know?

EVE: If I eat
And if I die

Will you die too?
WOMAN: If I eat
And if I die
Will you die too?

SERPENT 1: If you die
I will die too.

EVE: Why do you want me to eat?
WOMAN: Why do you want me to eat?

SERPENT 5: Because I want
SERPENT 4: I want to
SERPENT 3: I want to know.

EVE: Know what?
WOMAN: Know what?

SERPENT 2: Know what you will know.
SERPENT 1: Know what will happen.

EVE: I might.
I might do it.
I might do it if God didn't know.
WOMAN: I might.

I might do it.
I might do it if God didn't know.

SERPENT 3: You might
SERPENT 4: Might do it if God didn't know?
SERPENT 2: But you want to.
SERPENT 1: And he knows you want to.
SERPENT 5: Is a crime
SERPENT 4: Only a crime
SERPENT 5: When you're caught?

EVE: Shall I do what I want to then?
WOMAN: Shall I do what I want to then?

SERPENT 1 AND 2 AND 3 AND 4 AND 5: Yes!

EVE: Even if what I want is to listen
To God and not to you?

WOMAN: Even if what I want is to listen
To God and not to you?

SERPENT 1: Yes.
SERPENT 2: If you want.
SERPENT 3 AND 4: If you want.
SERPENT 5: Yes.

EVE: Then I will eat.
WOMAN: Then I will eat.

She bites into one of the apples held by the many hands of the serpent.

EVE: Because I want to.
WOMAN: Because I want to.

Eating the Apple

When Eve finally eats she is seated in the middle of the serpent. After a couple of frantic bites, there is a pause as Eve begins to savor the experience. The first woman of the chorus, who echoed Eve's words to the serpent, now describes Eve's experience.

FIRST WOMAN OF THE CHORUS

And Eve looked
At the creatures in the garden,
And at the ground
And at the wind and the water,
And she said: I am not the same as these.
And she began to examine
Her skin and her eyes
And her ears and her nose and her mouth.
And she began to examine her own mind.
And Eve went to Adam
To persuade him to eat.
But Adam said:

"You have eaten of that which was forbidden, and you shall die.
Do you want me to eat and die too?"

Eve in a kind of frenzy has gone over to Adam, woken him up, and is trying to have him eat. He, at first, refuses but then is caught up in her frenzy and he eats too. After his first bite nothing seems to happen. The serpent freezes during Adam and Eve's argument but he has shared Eve's ecstasy. The three other women of the chorus "davenn" while the first woman describes the action. This davenning is a rhythmic murmur like that of old women in churches and synagogues as they repeat and repeat familiar prayers and laments.

FIRST WOMAN OF THE CHORUS

But Adam ate.
And Adam looked
At the creatures in the garden,
And at the ground
And at the wind and the water,
And he said: I am not the same as these.
And he began to examine
His skin and his eyes
And his ears and his nose and his mouth.

34

And he began to examine his own mind.
And he could neither spit out the fruit
Nor could he swallow it.

Adam takes a second bite. All the actors, in a kind of ecstasy, form the serpent, moving in the same manner as we saw the serpent move with fewer actors earlier. The serpent, as played by all the actors, is still a display of the tree of life. It is seductive and inviting. Then the serpent separates.

A bag of apples is found on one side of the stage. An actor empties it out on the stage. The actors play with the apples, eat them, and carry them out to the audience to share their pleasure with them.

The Curses

Adam begins to cough a little. It is clear that he can indeed neither swallow the fruit nor spit it out. Suddenly, an actor who has been playing one of the creatures in the garden pulls Adam up from under the arms. Adam himself speaks for God when God is speaking to Adam. When speaking for God, Adam uses a voice which is larger and more resonant than his usual one, and the actor who lifts him mouths the same words. Adam's own attitude, as he speaks for God, is one of surprise and dismay. Whenever God will speak, all the actors on stage will whisper his words too.

GOD (*speaking through Adam*)
Where are you?

The actor who had lifted Adam up now drops him and goes back to playing a creature in the garden. Adam tries to hide, and he tries to cough up the fruit to be able to speak clearly to God. But the fruit remains stuck in his throat. The same actor picks him up again.

GOD (*speaking through Adam*)
Where are you?
Why do you not answer me?

The actor lets Adam drop and becomes a creature in the garden again.

ADAM (*answering God*)
I hear your voice in the garden
And I am afraid.

Adam is picked up again. Whenever he is picked up to speak, his body goes limp.

GOD (*speaking through Adam*)
Before
When you heard my voice
You were not afraid,
Yet, now you are afraid.

Adam is dropped again.

ADAM (*answering God*)

I am afraid
Because I am naked
And I have hidden myself.

Adam is picked up again from under the arms.

GOD (*speaking through Adam*)

Who told you
You were naked?
Have you eaten of the tree
From which
I commanded you not to eat?

Adam is dropped.

ADAM (*answering*)

Lord, so long as I was alone
I did not fall into sin.
But as soon as this woman came
She tempted me.

Another actor now lifts up Eve in the same way
Adam was lifted, and Eve is limp and speaks for
God in a voice that is larger and more resonant than

her usual one. The actor who lifts her, and the others, whisper the same words she is speaking.

GOD (*speaking through Eve*)
Woman, have you eaten of the tree
Whereof I commanded you not to eat?

Eve is let drop, and the actor who had lifted her goes back to playing a creature in the garden.

EVE (*answering God*)
It was the serpent, Lord.
He tempted me, and I ate.

SERPENT 1: You gave them a command,
and I contradicted it.
SERPENT 2: Why did they obey me
And not you?

From now on the voice of God is heard similarly through the different actors on the stage. All, except the four women of the chorus, lift each other in turn and speak with a voice that is larger than their usual ones. After lifting or being lifted, the actors return to being creatures in the garden. As the curses continue, there is a shorter space of time between them, and greater agitation in the garden. And as the curses are spoken each by one actor, the other actors simultaneously whisper them to the audience.

GOD (*speaking through one actor who is lifted from under his arms by another actor*)
Because you have done this
You are cursed over all animals.
Upon your belly shall you go
And dust shall you eat.

GOD (*speaking through another actor*)
Because you have eaten
Of the tree of which I commanded you,
Saying: You shall not eat of it,
Cursed is the earth for your sake.

GOD (*speaking through another actor*)
You shall use your mind
Not to understand but to doubt.
And even if you understand,
Still shall you doubt.

GOD (*speaking through another actor*)
When your children shall be found to murder,

You shall make laws.
But these laws shall not bind.

      GOD (*speaking through another actor*)
You shall be made to think,
And although few of your thoughts shall exalt you,
Many of your thoughts shall bring you sorrow,
And cause you to forget your exaltation.

      GOD (*speaking through another actor*)
Now shall come a separation
Between the dreams inside your head
And those things which you believe
To be outside your head
And the two shall war within you.

      GOD (*speaking through another actor*)
Accursed, you shall be alone.
For whatever you think,
And whatever you see or hear,
You shall think it and see it and hear it, alone.
Henceforth shall you thirst after me.

      GOD (*speaking through another actor*)
In the day shall you endure
The same longing as in the night,

And in the night shall you endure
The same longing as in the day.
Henceforth shall you thirst after me.

     GOD (*speaking through another actor*)
And your children shall live in fear of me.
And your children shall live in fear of you,
And your children shall live in fear of each other.

     GOD (*speaking through another actor*)
Accursed, you shall glimpse Eden
All the days of your life.
But you shall not come again.
And if you should come,
You would not know it.

     GOD (*speaking through another actor*)
And in the end
The earth shall wax old like a garment
And be cast off by me.

     GOD (*speaking through another actor*)
For that you were not able to observe the command
Laid upon you, for more than one hour,
Accursed be your days.
Henceforth shall you thirst after me.

         *   *   *

With the volume increasing, the curses begin to overlap. They are repeated and fragmented, spoken and whispered louder by an increasing number of actors. Many actors are regularly picked up and dropped. It becomes increasingly impossible to distinguish whole phrases. All the voices build into a frenzy and a din of sound.

And in the day
Shall you endure the same longing
As in the night.

Henceforth shall you thirst after me.

And in the night
Shall you endure the same longing
As in the day.

Henceforth shall you thirst after me.

And now shall come a separation.

Accursed.

Between the dreams inside your head.

43

Accursed.

And those things which you believe to be outside
    your head
And the two shall war within you.

And your children shall live in fear of me.

And in the end the earth shall wax old like a garment

And be cast off by me.

And your children shall live in fear of you.

You shall not come again to Eden.

And your children shall live in fear of each other.

And if you should come, you would not know it.

Accursed, you shall be made to think.

Accursed, you shall be alone.

And even when you understand,
Still shall you doubt.

44

Accursed.

Accursed.

Accursed.

Suddenly, there is silence. All the actors remain frozen a few seconds. Then Adam and Eve repeat, and continue to repeat throughout the next scene, their "locked" action of, respectively, accusing, and of reaching and subsiding.

Statements I

The four women are still kneeling.

In the beginning anything is possible.

SECOND WOMAN OF THE CHORUS
I've lost the beginning.

THIRD WOMAN OF THE CHORUS
I'm in the middle.

FOURTH WOMAN OF THE CHORUS
Knowing neither the end nor the beginning.

Now they stand. They sway slightly from side to side.

FIRST WOMAN
One lemming.

47

SECOND WOMAN

One lemming.

THIRD WOMAN

One lemming.

FOURTH WOMAN

One lemming.

When they are not speaking their own statements each of the women continues to say softly "one lemming" as an accompaniment to what the others are saying.

FIRST WOMAN

I try sometimes to imagine what it's like to be some-body else.

But it's always me pretending.

It has to be me.

Who else is there?

SECOND WOMAN

I hugged my child
And sent him off to school
With his lunch in a paper bag.
And I wished he would never come home.

48

THIRD WOMAN

I'm concerned
Because what you reject
Can still run your life.

FOURTH WOMAN

I passed my friend on the street.

SECOND WOMAN

I passed quite near.

FOURTH WOMAN

I don't think she saw me.
If she did, I don't think

SECOND WOMAN

She saw me see her.

FOURTH WOMAN

I think she thought

SECOND WOMAN

If she saw me

FOURTH WOMAN

That I didn't see her.

49

THIRD WOMAN

If God exists
It is through me.
And He will protect me
Because He owes His existence to me.

FIRST WOMAN

Old stories
Have a secret.

SECOND WOMAN

They are a prison.

THIRD WOMAN

Someone is locked inside them.

FOURTH WOMAN

Sometimes, when it's very quiet,
I can hear him breathing.

SECOND WOMAN

Sometimes I feel there's nothing to do
But help other people.
But as soon as I join a committee or a party
I know that has nothing to do with it at all.

50

FOURTH WOMAN

Whatever I know

SECOND WOMAN

I know it without words.

FOURTH WOMAN

I am here as a witness.

SECOND WOMAN

To what?

FOURTH WOMAN

I don't know.

THIRD WOMAN

It was different when I was a child.
I don't see any more bright colors.
There are no solid blocks
Or familiar rooms.

FIRST WOMAN

I went to a dinner.
The guests were pleasant.
We were poised,

Smiling over our plates,

Asking and answering the usual questions.

I wanted to throw the food,

Ax the table,

Scratch the women's faces,

And grab the men's balls.

SECOND WOMAN

When asked, I blamed it on the other person.

It wasn't me, I said.

It must have been her.

I could have said it was me,

But I said it was her.

THIRD WOMAN

My home was Cleveland.

Then I came to New York

And I didn't have to account to anybody.

I smoked: pot, hashish, opium.

I slept with a man.

I slept with a woman.

I slept with a man and a woman at the same time.

But I'm a gentle person, and I collapsed.

FOURTH WOMAN

I'm still a child.

53

SECOND WOMAN

So am I.

FOURTH WOMAN

Sometimes people nod at you,
And smile,
And you know they haven't heard.

FIRST WOMAN

On a certain day

SECOND WOMAN

Of a certain year

THIRD WOMAN

One lemming

FOURTH WOMAN

Starts to run.

FIRST WOMAN

Another lemming, seeing the first,

SECOND WOMAN

Drops everything,

54

THIRD WOMAN

And starts to run too.

FOURTH WOMAN

Little by little

FIRST WOMAN

All the lemmings

SECOND WOMAN

From all over the country

THIRD WOMAN

Run together

FOURTH WOMAN

For tens

FIRST WOMAN

And hundreds of miles

SECOND WOMAN

Until,

FOURTH WOMAN

Exhausted,

FIRST WOMAN

They reach the cliff

SECOND WOMAN

And throw themselves

THIRD WOMAN

Into the sea.

Cain and Abel

The four women continue to davenn, but now without words, except when indicated. Davenning-without-words is like a rhythmic humming, and it continues under the voices of the individual women who are speaking. Cain chops wood. Abel tends two sheep. The scene begins slowly to unfold between them. It will continue beyond the recital of the action by the chorus.

FOURTH WOMAN

And when they were cast out
Eve and Adam remembered me.
And Eve conceived
And bore Cain,
And she said:

FOURTH AND SECOND WOMEN

"Lo, I have gotten
A man from the Lord."

FOURTH WOMAN

And again Adam and Eve remembered me.
And Eve bore Abel.
And again she said:

FOURTH AND SECOND WOMEN

"Lo, I have gotten
A man from the Lord."

FOURTH WOMAN

Then Eve had a dream,
And she ran and told it to Adam.
And Eve said:
"Lo, I saw Adam's blood flow from Cain's mouth."
And wishing to divert any evil that might come,
Adam separated Cain from Abel.
And Cain became a tiller of the ground,
And Abel a keeper of sheep.
And in time Cain offered unto the Lord
A sacrifice of first fruits,
While his brother Abel offered a firstborn lamb.
And the Lord had love for Abel and for his offering.
But for Cain and for his offering
The Lord had no respect.
And Cain said:

FOURTH AND FIRST WOMEN

"Why did He accept your offering
And not mine?"

FOURTH WOMAN

And Cain's face grew dark,
And his words were not pleasing to the Lord,
And Cain said:

FOURTH AND FIRST WOMEN

"Why did He accept your offering
And not mine?"

FOURTH WOMAN

"There is no law
And there is no judge."
And the Lord spoke within him,
And He said:
"If you will amend your ways
I will forgive your anger.
Yet even now the power of evil
Crouches at the door."
But it occurred to Cain
That the world was created through goodness,
Yet he saw that good deeds bear no fruit.

And God said:
"It depends on you
Whether you shall be master over evil,
Or evil over you."
And Cain said:

FOURTH AND FIRST WOMEN
"Why did He accept your offering
And not mine?"

FOURTH WOMAN
And it occurred to Cain
That the world
Is ruled with an arbitrary power.
And Cain said:
"There is no law and there is no judge."

FOURTH AND FIRST WOMEN
"Else
Why did He not accept my offering,
Yet He accepted yours?"

FOURTH WOMAN
And it occurred to Cain
To kill his brother.
But it did not occur to Cain

That killing his brother
Would cause his brother's death.
For Cain did not know how to kill
And he struck at his brother.
And broke each of his bones in turn
And this was the first murder.
And Cain said:
"If I were to spill your blood on the ground
As you do the sheep's,
Who is there to demand it of me?"
And Abel said:
"The Lord will demand it. The Lord will judge."
And Cain said:
"There is no judge. There is no law."

FOURTH AND FIRST WOMEN

"Else
Why did He accept your offering
And not accept mine?"

FOURTH WOMAN

"Why yours?
Why not mine?"
And it occurred to Cain
To kill his brother.
But it did not occur to Cain

61

That killing his brother
Would cause his brother's death.
For Cain did not know how to kill.
And he struck at his brother
And broke each of his bones in turn.
And Abel said: "The Lord will judge."
And Cain said:
"There is no judge. There is no law."

FOURTH AND FIRST WOMEN

"Else
Why did he accept your offering
And not accept mine?"

FOURTH WOMAN

"Why yours?
Why not mine?"
And this was the first murder.
For it occurred to Cain
To kill his brother.
But it did not occur to Cain
That killing his brother
Would cause his brother's death.

Cain has come over to Abel. He feeds Abel's sheep,
to get them out of his way. He looks at Abel, and

62

Abel looks back at Cain. The rest of the actors, not including the chorus, breathe together regularly and quietly—they are breathing Abel's breath. Cain tries different ways of killing Abel. After trying each different way, he looks at Abel to see the result of what he has done, and to try to decide what to do next. The rest of the company watches, and the sheep remain quietly by. Some of the things that Cain does to Abel are to pull at his limbs, to hold him in the air and think of dashing him on the ground. Finally, he lays Abel down on the ground, and seeing that there is still movement in the respiratory area, Cain uses his hands to chop at Abel's throat. Abel's breathing stops. All the sounds for hurting Abel and for the chopping at him with his hands have come from the actor playing Cain, rather than from the actor playing Abel. Now Cain listens for Abel's breathing, which he misses hearing. He tries to breathe breath back into Abel from his own mouth. Then he tries to stand Abel up. He puts grass into his lifeless hand to try to have Abel feed the sheep. Finally, he lays Abel down on the backs of his two sheep, standing behind him, swaying slightly from side to side, waiting, waiting for life to start up again in Abel. The heron from the garden is back, and it wanders near, making its

gentle noise and standing on one leg and then the other. Cain continues to wait. The four women of the chorus make a small, long screeching sound from the backs of their throats. Abel, as a ghost, now crawls on his knees toward the front of the stage. He confronts the audience. The actor playing Abel is, at this moment, experiencing extreme tension throughout his body, and reseeing in his mind's eye what just happened to him. Cain, still watching the place where he put Abel's body on the sheep, continues to wait.

Blind Men's Hell

The two actors who played the sheep, and one other actor, are on their backs on the floor. All the others, with the exception of the chorus, walk around and through them. All are blind and as if experiencing tremendous fatigue. They are like people who have lived too long. None of those who are walking may stop or fall—if they do, they must immediately get up and go on. Those on the floor grope upward, grabbing at parts of the moving people. This continues during Statements II.

Statements II

In the beginning
Anything is possible.
From the center
I can choose to go anywhere.

SECOND WOMAN OF THE CHORUS
But now the point
Toward which I have chosen to go
Has a line drawn
Between itself
And the beginning.

FOURTH WOMAN OF THE CHORUS
I no longer know the beginning.
I am in the middle.
On a line
Between the beginning
And a point toward which I chose to go.

THIRD WOMAN OF THE CHORUS

I have fewer choices now.
Because when I change my direction
The change can only start
From a line already drawn.
Now the four women smile. They keep smiling
unless they are speaking. They sway slightly from
side to side.

SECOND WOMAN

I'm collecting things.
Beads.
I'm buying plants,
Curtains—
With which to make a home.
I'm buying things
To make a good life.

THIRD WOMAN

When I was thirteen
I wanted a house of my own.
The girl I was then
Would say to me now:
"What have you done with your advantages?"
You could have married a rich man,
And had a big house.
Instead, you're a freak."

FIRST WOMAN (*as the other women and herself open and close one fist*)
Open.
Close.
Open.
Close.
No effort
Makes these two movements
One.

SECOND WOMAN
My husband is in that coffin.
In the day he goes to work.
In the evening we discuss household matters.
And at night
He climbs back into the coffin.

THIRD WOMAN
Even if you sit and do nothing,
Even so,
Your back is strapped to a wheel,
And the wheel turns.

FOURTH WOMAN
While we were in bed I asked a boy,

SECOND WOMAN

I asked him if he should be around

FIRST WOMAN

If he should be around when I die,
Would he hold and rock me in his arms
For half an hour afterwards.

THIRD WOMAN

Because they can't tell.

FOURTH WOMAN

They can only approximate.

SECOND WOMAN

They can't tell when you're really dead.

FIRST WOMAN

Not exactly.

THIRD WOMAN

Not the exact moment.

SECOND WOMAN

When I was a child
This story was told to me in secret by a friend:
"A little boy came into his mother's room

71

And saw her naked.
'What's that?' he asked.
'It's a wound,' she said.
'What happened to your penis?' he asked.
'Oh,' she said,
'God chopped it off with an ax.' "

THIRD WOMAN (*with other women speaking
and emphasizing the words "he," "his," and
him"*)
It's my husband.
He keeps me from it.
It's *his* fault.
He keeps me down, holds me at *his* level.
I could be happy
If it weren't for *him*.

FOURTH WOMAN
The doctors lie.
My mother died screaming with pain.
Did you know you could go into eternity
Screaming with pain?

FIRST WOMAN (*as the other women and herself
open and close one fist*)
Open.
Close.

Separate movements.
Stretched-out fingers.
Nails into skin.
One to open.
One to close.
Separate
Motions.
No matter how I try,
These movements
Are not one.
There is a stop between open
And close, and between close
And open.
No effort
Makes these two movements
One.
Close.
Open.
Close.

SECOND WOMAN
You can see them having lunch,

FIRST WOMAN
Their faces pale,

73

THIRD WOMAN

Laughing.
They are corpses laughing.

FOURTH WOMAN

You can see them on the streets,

SECOND WOMAN

Combed and brushed.

FIRST WOMAN

They are colored pictures.

FIRST AND THIRD WOMEN

The men have killed each other.

SECOND AND FOURTH WOMEN

The king is dead.

FOURTH WOMAN

He was shot in the head.

FIRST WOMAN

By an unknown assassin.

74

SECOND WOMAN

The men are dead.

THIRD WOMAN

And no man can say
Of work or land:
"This is mine."

FIRST AND SECOND WOMEN

The men are dead.

SECOND WOMAN

We mourn them.

THIRD AND FOURTH WOMEN

We are dead.

THIRD WOMAN

We mourn ourselves.

FOURTH WOMAN

If a bulldog ant
Is cut in two,
A battle starts
Between the head and the tail.

75

The head bites the tail.
The tail stings the head.
They fight
Until both halves are dead.

THIRD WOMAN

So Man created God.
What for?
To set limits on himself.

FIRST WOMAN

Would my dreams recognize me?
Would they come to me and say
"She's the one who imagined us"?

THIRD WOMAN

I was queen over a country
Where the air was sweet.
We ate honey and fruit.
And at night
It was quiet.

SECOND WOMAN

Suddenly—
This moment.
Here, now.

I am here,
And you.
In this place, now
We are together.

> FIRST WOMAN (*as the other three women, and finally she, begin to make the body sounds of the entering procession*)

At the very end.
Even after the end,
Even when the body is on its own,
The human being can make such a variety
Of sounds that it's amazing.
A field of dead men is loud.
Teeth clack, bones crack,
Limbs twist and drop,
And the last sound of all
Is a loud trumpet
Of escaping wind.

Begatting

Now all together the four women begin davenning again, for a moment without words. The Blind Men's Hell has dissolved. Two actors, a man and a woman, begin very slowly approaching each other from either side of the stage. The four women are kneeling and rocking back and forth. All the others begin gently to explore each other's bodies.

THIRD WOMAN (*as the other three davenn under her words*)
And Adam knew Eve and Eve knew Adam
And this was the first time.
And Adam knew Eve and Eve knew Adam
And this was the first time.

The actors are exploring each other's bodies as if for the first time. The women now open a book and read the "begats" from the Old Testament of the Bible. Each woman reads some part and then passes the book to another. But all are continually davenning and, frequently, the exact words of the begatting are lost in favor of the rhythmic davenning and the rocking back and forth toward the audience.

THIRD WOMAN (*reading*)

And Adam lived a hundred and thirty years and he begat a son in his own likeness and he called his name Seth.

And the days of Adam after he had begotten Seth were eight hundred years, and he begat sons and daughters.

And Seth lived a hundred and five years and he begat Enos.

And Seth lived after he begat Enos eight hundred and seven years, and he begat sons and daughters.

And Enos lived ninety years and he begat Cainan.

And Enos lived after he begat Cainan eight hundred and fifteen years, and he begat sons and daughters.

And Cainan lived seventy years and begat Mahalaleel.

The man and woman come closer and closer to touching. The others have paired off, too, and are still exploring bodies.

FOURTH WOMAN (*reading*)

And Cainan lived, after he begat Mahalaleel, eight hundred and forty years, and he begat sons and daughters.

And Mahalaleel lived sixty and five years, and he begat Jared.

And Mahalaleel lived, after he begat Jared, eight hundred and thirty years, and he begat sons and daughters.

And Jared lived a hundred and sixty and two years, and he begat Enoch.

And Jared lived after he begat Enoch eight hundred years, and he begat sons and daughters.

And Enoch lived sixty and five years and he begat Methuselah.

And Enoch walked with God after he begat Methuselah three hundred years, and he begat sons and daughters.

And Enoch walked with God and he was not, for God took him.

And Methuselah lived a hundred and eighty and seven years, and he begat Lamech.

And Methuselah lived after he begat Lamech seven hundred and eighty and two years, and he begat sons and daughters.

And Lamech lived a hundred eighty and two years and he begat a son, and he called his name Noah.

And Lamech lived after he begat Noah five hundred and ninety years, and he begat sons and daughters.

And Noah was five hundred years old, and Noah begat Shem and Ham and Japheth.

By now, the two people have met in the center of the stage and embraced. All the couples are now exploring each other more gymnastically. They are

trying to find how to make the connection between the male and the female body. They try various difficult positions. Eventually all make the connection and they copulate in increasingly faster rhythm.

FIRST WOMAN (*reading*)

And these are the generations of the sons of Noah and Shem and Ham and Japheth and the sons that were born to them after the flood:

The sons of Japheth were Gomer and Magog and Madai and Javan and Tubal and Meshech and Tiras.

And the sons of Gomer were Ashkenaz and Riphath and Togarmah.

And the sons of Javan were Elishah and Tarshish and Kittim and Dodanim.

And the sons of Ham were Cush and Mizraim and Phut and Canaan.

And the sons of Cush were Seba and Havilah and Sabtah and Raamah and Sabtechah.

And the sons of Raamah were Sheba and Dedan.

And Cush begat Nimrod, and he began to be a mighty one on earth.

And Canaan begat Sidon, his firstborn, and Heth.

And unto Shem were born Elam and Ashur and Arphaxad and Lud and Aram.

And the children of Aram were Uz and Hul and Gether and Mash.

And Arphaxad begat Salah, and Salah begat Eber.

82

And unto Eber were born two sons, and one was called Peleg, and his brother's name was Joktan.

And Joktan begat Almodad and Shelaph and Hazarmaveth and Jerah.

And Hadoram and Uzal and Diklah.

All the couples reach their climax at approximately the same time. Immediately afterward, the women go into labor, and they then give birth. Their sons are played by the actors who played their lovers. After the birth, the mothers teach their children how to talk, walk, play games, etc.

SECOND WOMAN (*reading*)

And Obal and Abimael and Sheba,
and Ophir and Havilah and Johab.
All these were the sons of Joktan.

And these were the generations of Shem.

Shem was a hundred years old and begat Arphaxad two years after the flood.

And Shem lived after he begat Arphaxad five hundred years, and he begat sons and daughters.

And Arphaxad lived five and thirty years and he begat Salah.

And Arphaxad lived after he begat Salah four hundred and three years, and he begat sons and daughters.

And Salah lived thirty years and he begat Eber.

And Salah lived after he begat Eber four hundred and three years, and he begat sons and daughters.

83

And Eber lived four hundred and thirty years and he begat Peleg.

And Eber lived after he begat Peleg four hundred and thirty years, and he begat sons and daughters.

And Peleg lived thirty years and he begat Reu.

And Peleg lived after he begat Reu two hundred and nine years, and he begat sons and daughters.

And Reu lived thirty and two years, and he begat Serug.

And Reu lived after he begat Serug two hundred and seven years, and he begat sons and daughters.

And Serug lived thirty years and he begat Nahor.

And Serug lived after he begat Nahor two hundred years, and he begat sons and daughters.

And Nahor lived twenty and nine years, and he begat Terah.

And Nahor lived after he begat Terah a hundred and nineteen years and he begat sons and daughters.

And Terah lived seventy years, and he begat Abram and Nahor and Haran.

And these are the generations of Terah.

From being small children, the men of the company have become very old people. They are brought forward, helped slowly, to the front of the stage by their mothers, who have remained young. One or two of the actresses play old women and also stay at the front of the stage.

THIRD WOMAN (*reading*)

Terah begat Isaac, and Isaac begat Jacob and Jacob begat Judah and his brethren.

And Judah begat Phares and Zarah, of Thamar.

And Phares begat Esrom.

And Esrom begat Aram.

And Aram begat Aminadab.

And Aminadab begat Naasson.

And Naasson begat Salmon.

And Salmon begat Booz, of Rachab.

And Booz begat Obed, of Ruth.

And Obed begat Jesse.

And Jesse begat David the king.

And David the king begat Solomon, of her that had been the wife of Urias.

And Solomon begat Rehoboam.

And Rehoboam begat Abia.

And Abia begat Asa.

And Asa begat Josaphat.

And Josaphat begat Joram.

And Joram begat Ozias.

And Ozias begat Joatham.

And Joatham begat Achaz.

And Achaz begat Ezekias.

And Ezekias begat Manasses.

And Manasses begat Amon.

And Amon begat Josias.

And Josias begat Jechonias and his brethren about the time they were carried away to Babylon.

And after they were brought to Babylon, Jechonias begat Salathiel.

And Salathiel begat Zorobabel.

And Zorobabel begat Abiud.

And Abiud begat Eliakim.

And Eliakim begat Azor.

And Azor begat Sadoc.

And Sadoc begat Achim.

And Achim begat Eliud.

And Eliud begat Eleazur.

And Eleazur begat Mathan.

And Mathan begat Jacob.

And Jacob begat Joseph.

Old People

There is now a line of old people facing the audience at the front of the stage. They speak out a name or two, or mumble, from the many names of the "begatting." The four women of the chorus are davenning without words. The other actresses, the ones who have just played the mothers, are at the back of the stage, and they davenn, too, softly.

The Song

The actors move about freely on the stage. Each is overtaken by a slow kind of dying, not so much a physical one as a kind of "emptying out," a living death which soon slows them to a complete stop. Each actor has a final small physical tremor. Then, as if ghosts, the actors begin to sing a sentimental popular song from twenty or thirty years ago. No longer as ghosts but as themselves they continue singing the song as they leave the theater, walking out through the audience.

Jean-Claude van Itallie

Jean-Claude van Itallie was born in Brussels in 1936. He was raised on Long Island, in Great Neck, and graduated from Harvard in 1958. He joined the Open Theater when it started, in 1963. In November 1966 his *America Hurrah* opened at the Pocket Theater in New York and ran there for over one and a half years. It has since been produced, hailed, and banned all over the world.

The Open Theater

In 1963 a group of actors and directors and playwrights in downtown New York found themselves at the same point in their professional development—tired of conventional New York theatrical expression, and disgusted with the nearly total lack of outlets available for experimental work. This group, headed by Joseph Chaikin, became the Open Theater. The nucleus of the group is the same five years later. And their dialogue continues about what is worth expressing in the theater, and how to express it. The Open Theater has been deliberately non-commercial. Rent on the rehearsal loft has been paid by members' dues. But the Open Theater has, since its beginning, performed one- or two-night programs of short plays and improvisations in nearly every off and off-off-Broadway house. And its effect on all phases of avant-garde American theater, to quote the *Village Voice,* "has been seminal." *The Serpent* is the first piece to be built fully as a collaborative work within and by the Open Theater. It is the result of several months' unpaid, full-time commitment, and countless discussions and improvisations on the part of the eighteen actors and the other artists involved. *The Serpent* was taken to Europe by the Open Theater in the summer of 1968, and it was enthusiastically received there by audiences and critics in Italy, Switzerland, Germany and Denmark.

Joseph Chaikin

Joseph Chaikin, founder of the Open Theater, is thirty-two years old. He was born in Brooklyn of Russian parents, and he went to school at Drake University in Iowa. He was for several years the central actor of the Living Theater, with which the Open Theater has continued to exchange ideas over the years. Chaikin has won several off-Broadway "Obies," including one for his performance in Brecht's *Man Is Man*.